ICONIC AMERICA

# HOLLYWOOD

BY ALEXIS BURLING

CONTENT CONSULTANT
J. E. Smyth, PhD
Professor of History
University of Warwick

Cover image: Hollywood Boulevard is a busy and bustling street in Hollywood, California.

Core Library
An Imprint of Abdo Publishing
abdobooks.com

abdobooks.com

Published by Abdo Publishing, a division of ABDO, PO Box 398166, Minneapolis, Minnesota 55439. 

Printed in the United States of America, North Mankato, Minnesota
092019
012020

Cover Photo: View Apart/Shutterstock Images
Interior Photos: View Apart/Shutterstock Images, 1; Shutterstock Images, 4–5; iStockphoto, 8; Mike Blake/Reuters/Newscom, 10–11; Angel DiBilio/Shutterstock Images, 12; Alfred Eisenstaedt/Pix Inc./The LIFE Picture Collection/Getty Images, 15; Hulton Archive/Archive Photos/Getty Images, 18–19; Sean Pavone/Shutterstock Images, 23, 45; akg-images/Newscom, 26–27, 43; Paramount Pictures/Album/Newscom, 32; Ingus Kruklitis/Shutterstock Images, 34–35; Red Line Editorial, 37; Faye Sadou/MediaPunch/IPX/AP Images, 40

Editor: Maddie Spalding
Series Designer: Claire Vanden Branden

**Library of Congress Control Number: 2019942268**

**Publisher's Cataloging-in-Publication Data**

Names: Burling, Alexis, author.
Title: Hollywood / by Alexis Burling
Description: Minneapolis, Minnesota : Abdo Publishing, 2020 | Series: Iconic America | Includes online resources and index.
Identifiers: ISBN 9781532190902 (lib. bdg.) | ISBN 9781532176753 (ebook)
Subjects: LCSH: Hollywood (Los Angeles, Calif.)--History--Juvenile literature. | Motion picture industry--Juvenile literature. | Celebrities--United States--Juvenile literature. | Movie stars--Juvenile literature. | Chinese Theatre (Los Angeles, Calif.)--Juvenile literature.
Classification: DDC 917.9494--dc23

# CONTENTS

# CHAPTER ONE

# THE ACADEMY AWARDS

On February 24, 2019, millions of people around the world took part in a yearly tradition. Families and friends gathered together in their living rooms. They popped bowls of buttery popcorn. Then they turned on their televisions to watch the ninety-first Academy Awards.

The Academy Awards show happens each year in Hollywood, California. Hollywood is a district within the city of Los Angeles. It has been the center of the US film industry for more than 100 years. The Academy of Motion Picture Arts and Sciences was founded

**Actors Mahershala Ali, *left*, and Regina King, *right*, won Oscars at the 2019 Academy Awards.**

in 1927. The Academy supports and honors film industry professionals. It has approximately 9,000 members. They vote to award golden trophies called Oscars for the best achievements in the movie industry. Early Academy Awards shows were broadcast live on the radio. The first televised Academy Awards show aired on March 19, 1953.

The ninety-first Academy Awards ceremony was full of surprises. Unlike in the past 30 years, the show did not have a host.

## THE DOLBY THEATRE

**The Dolby Theatre has hosted the Academy Awards ceremony since 2002. Other musical and theater performances are also held there. Musicians Alicia Keys, Prince, and Stevie Wonder have performed at the theater. Visitors can take a guided tour of the building. Outside, there is an Awards Walk that spans two stories. It includes glass plaques for every best picture Academy Award winner. Inside, there is a large lobby with a spiral staircase. The Dolby Theatre's stage is one of the largest in the United States.**

Some of the awards were unexpected too. The movie *Green Book* won the best picture award. Many people were upset by this. They did not think the movie portrayed black musician Don Shirley accurately. But overall, the experience was magical. For many people in the film industry, being part of the Academy Awards is one of the top honors of their career.

## BEFORE THE SHOW

The Academy Awards is an exciting event to watch at home. But the real action happens in Hollywood's Dolby Theatre. The show is held in this theater.

Before the show, elegantly dressed celebrities walk down a red carpet outside the theater. Thousands of people travel to Hollywood to see the celebrities walk the carpet. They stand along Hollywood Boulevard. Some even win a chance to sit in the bleachers near the entrance to the Dolby Theatre.

## HOLLYWOOD MAP

This map shows where Hollywood is located. It also shows some of Hollywood's famous attractions. Most are near the intersection of Hollywood Boulevard and Vine Street. How does this map help you better understand the layout of Hollywood?

## CITY OF DREAMS

The Academy Awards is not the only attraction that brings people to Hollywood. The Hollywood Walk of Fame is a popular landmark. It is a long stretch of sidewalk that runs along Hollywood Boulevard. On the sidewalk are more than 2,600 stars. Each star has the name of an important person in the entertainment industries. Another attraction is the Hollywood Museum. It has a collection of more than 10,000 items. The museum explores the history of Hollywood's film industry.

Today, Hollywood is a thriving place full of culture. It is also known for its fascinating past. Hollywood landmarks have rich histories. They tell the story of an ever-changing place where dreams are born.

## PERSPECTIVES

### THE RED CARPET

**One of the most recognizable parts of the Academy Awards ceremony is the red carpet. It is 500 feet (150 m) long. A red carpet first appeared at the Academy Awards in 1961. Hollywood historian Marc Wanamaker said the carpet had many purposes. He explained, "The first purpose is that it would be an obvious guideline of where people would walk. The other reason is that they didn't want anyone slipping or falling going into the theater. The third reason is that it is glamorous."**

CHAPTER TWO

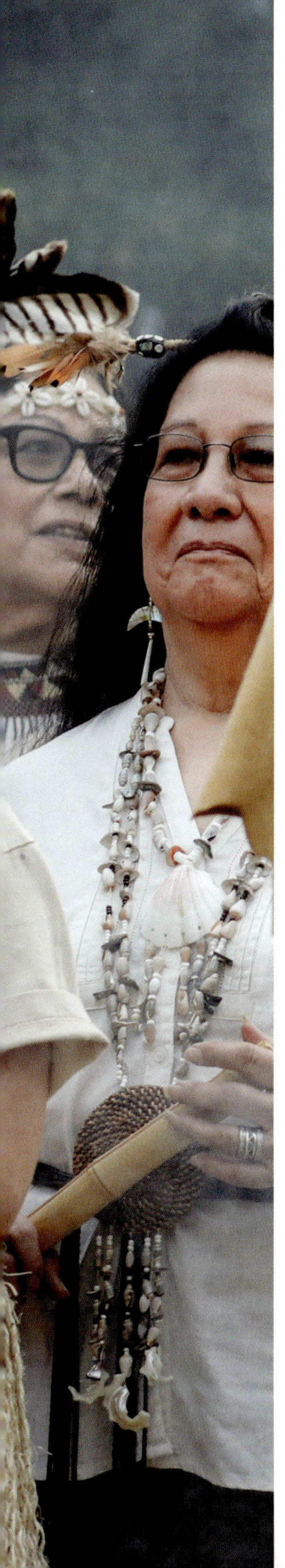

# EARLY HISTORY

Today, Hollywood is full of busy roads and tall buildings. But this has not always been the case. Originally, the area was home to the Tongva Native Americans. The Tongva settled in the present-day Los Angeles Basin. Approximately 5,000 Tongva lived in nearly 100 villages before European settlers arrived. Today, approximately 2,000 people are descendants of the Tongva. Some location names in California, such as Cahuenga and Topanga, come from words in the Tongva's native language.

In the mid-1700s, Spanish people invaded the area. Spanish soldiers and priests took the Tongva's land. They founded Roman Catholic

**Today, Tongva Native Americans continue to celebrate their culture and heritage.**

The San Gabriel Arcángel mission was founded in 1771.

missions such as San Gabriel Arcángel. Priests enslaved the Tongva people. They forced the Tongva to build and work for their missions. They made Tongva people convert to Christianity. The Spanish also carried diseases. The Spanish were used to these diseases so were mostly unaffected by them. But this was the first time the Tongva had been exposed to these diseases. Many died from illness. The settlers also enslaved

Tongva people. By the time new waves of settlers moved into California in the 1840s and 1850s, the Tongva's population had plummeted.

In 1850, California became a state. White Americans invaded and took Native peoples' lands. They too enslaved Native Americans and brought more disease. They also killed thousands of Native Americans. Between 1850 and 1900, California's Native American population declined by 95 percent.

## HOLLYWOOD'S BEGINNINGS

In 1883, businessman Harvey Henderson Wilcox and his wife, Daeida, settled in Los Angeles. They later bought land in the Cahuenga Valley. They owned 120 acres (49 ha). They planned to create a subdivision, or an area made up of plots of land that could be sold. They hired workers to plant pepper trees. They envisioned a neighborhood with streets and parks. Soon this neighborhood had a name: Hollywood. Land in Hollywood went up for sale in 1887.

Land in Hollywood was cheap. This drew many people to the area. They built homes along a street they called Prospect Avenue. After Harvey died in 1891, Daeida continued to expand the community. She wanted to create a Christian community. She offered free land to Christian churches. She also helped build schools, grocery stores, a library, and a post office. Soon the population of Hollywood had increased to more than 500 people.

PERSPECTIVES

### NAMING HOLLYWOOD

**Many people disagree on how Hollywood got its name. Some historians think Daeida came up with the name. They believe she was inspired by a beautiful mansion in Illinois called Hollywood. Other people think H. J. Whitley came up with the name when he visited the area in 1886. Still others say the town was named after the California Holly, a plant that grows in the area.**

## GROWTH AND DEVELOPMENT

In 1902, banker and real estate developer H. J. Whitley was drawn to Hollywood.

Land in Hollywood was valuable in the early 1900s.

He knew there would be many business opportunities in the growing community. He built the community's first hotel in 1903. It was called the Hollywood Hotel.

Whitley developed Hollywood in other ways too. He built a fancy neighborhood called Ocean View Tract. It brought in many wealthy homeowners. Whitley also helped to bring in electricity, gas for heating, and telephone service. Because of his contributions, some people call him the Father of Hollywood.

On November 14, 1903, Hollywood officially became a town. Prospect Avenue was renamed Hollywood Boulevard. Then in 1910, Hollywood merged with Los Angeles. Hollywood became a district within the larger city. At that time, more than 5,000 people lived in Hollywood.

### THE HOLLYWOOD HOTEL

**In the early 1900s, the Hollywood Hotel was a popular place to stay. It had a grand staircase, a children's dining room, a wraparound porch, and even a barber shop. Movie stars dined in the hotel's banquet room. Stars with the names of celebrities were painted on the ceiling of the banquet room. The room was called the Dining Room of the Stars. By the 1950s, the hotel had fallen into disrepair. It was torn down in 1956 to make way for an office building.**

## THE FILM INDUSTRY

A new but growing film industry soon drew many people to Hollywood. In the late 1800s, most movies were made in New York and New Jersey. But by the early 1900s, movie executives had started exploring California. They found cheaper land in Hollywood.

Directors also moved to Hollywood because the weather there was warm and sunny year-round. In October 1911, Hollywood's first film studio opened. It was called Nestor Motion Picture Company. The studio filmed its first movie on Whitley's ranch.

## FURTHER EVIDENCE

**Chapter Two explored some of California's Native American history. Identify one of the chapter's main points. What evidence does the author provide to support this point? Visit the website below to learn more about the Tongva. Does the information on the website support the point you identified? Does it present new evidence?**

### THE GABRIELINO-TONGVA TRIBE

**abdocorelibrary.com/hollywood**

# CHAPTER THREE

# HOLLYWOOD'S GOLDEN AGE

In the early 1900s, films were in black and white. At first, the films were often only a few minutes long. The camera did not move within a shot. These films did not have sound. Instead they showed intertitles. Intertitles were written words projected onto the screen. That way, audiences could know what the actors were saying. These films without sound were called silent films. But the viewing experience was not entirely silent. Many movies were accompanied by live music. In a movie theater, musicians played along to the film. Silent films starring Mary Pickford, Charlie Chaplin, and

**Dorothy Arzner, *left*, was a well-known Hollywood film director whose career spanned from the 1920s to the 1940s.**

Douglas Fairbanks were especially popular. By the 1910s, movies had become longer. They were more than an hour long. They were called feature-length films.

In the 1920s, Hollywood entered an era called the Golden Age. This period lasted through the 1960s. It was a time of great prosperity thanks to the growing film industry. Wealthy neighborhoods quickly cropped up around Hollywood.

## PERSPECTIVES

### WOMEN IN HOLLYWOOD

Mary Pickford was a famous actress in the early 1900s. She starred in silent films. She also became one of Hollywood's most influential executives. In 1919, she cofounded United Artists. Historian Cari Beauchamp said, "She didn't just accept being a star; she took that power and became a producer, became a company owner." Pickford was one of many women to hold positions of power in Hollywood. Directors Lois Weber and Dorothy Arzner, film editor Margaret Booth, and writer Mary C. McCall Jr. were other well-known Hollywood women. Bette Davis was elected President of the Academy of Motion Picture Arts and Sciences in 1941.

Many actors moved to the area. By the early 1920s, Hollywood produced most of the films shown in the United States.

## BUSINESS BOOM

The dawn of the Golden Age brought new film companies to Hollywood. Warner Bros., RKO Radio Pictures, Twentieth Century-Fox, Metro-Goldwyn-Mayer (MGM), and Paramount Pictures all opened in the area. They became the major film studios. They were known as the Big Five. Smaller film

## THE HOLLYWOOD SIGN

**One attraction that draws many tourists to Hollywood today is the Hollywood sign. This sign is made up of letters mounted on the hills above the city. Harry Chandler built this sign in 1923. Chandler was a real estate developer and the publisher of the *Los Angeles Times* newspaper. He wanted to advertise a new housing development in the area. His sign originally said "Hollywoodland." The sign was only supposed to be up for a few years. But it was restored in 1949, and part of the word was removed. Today the sign reads, "Hollywood."**

studios also opened. They included Columbia Pictures, Universal, and United Artists. Many studios had offices at the intersection of Hollywood Boulevard and Vine Street. For this reason, this intersection became famous.

Going to the movies became a popular pastime in Hollywood and around the country. Large, glamorous theaters were built to show movies to the public. These theaters were often called movie palaces. Showman Sid Grauman built two movie palaces in Hollywood: the Egyptian Theatre and the Chinese Theatre. The Egyptian Theatre held the first-ever movie premiere in 1922 for director Douglas Fairbanks's *Robin Hood*. The Chinese Theatre was opened in 1927. Today, it is known as the TCL Chinese Theatre. It remains a popular attraction in Hollywood today. The handprints and footprints of famous movie stars are displayed in the concrete outside the theater.

**Each year, approximately 4 million people visit the TCL Chinese Theatre.**

CHINESE THEATRE

## TALKIES

In the late 1920s, there was a major shift in the way films were made. Film producers began to add sound to their movies. They put soundtracks onto the film strips. These new types of films were called "talkies." The 1927 movie *The Jazz Singer* is widely known as the first talking feature film. By 1929, most of the movies made in Hollywood had some form of sound.

In the 1930s, film budgets continued to grow. Many studios spent thousands of dollars on color technology. They thought movies in color, called Technicolor films, would attract larger audiences. Technicolor films dated back to the 1910s. But studios began to make more Technicolor films in the 1930s. Popular movies such as *Gone with the Wind* were made in Technicolor.

In the 1930s, the United States was in the midst of the Great Depression. This was a period when many people were out of work. They did not have much money. But the cost to see a movie was fairly low.

The average cost to see a movie in 1933 was about a quarter. Movies were popular because they helped people escape the stress of their daily lives.

Between 1930 and 1945, Hollywood studios made more than 7,500 films. Producers experimented with new types of movies, including documentaries, comedies, and horror films. Hollywood's film industry thrived.

## EXPLORE ONLINE

**Chapter Three discusses the Golden Age of Hollywood. The website below explores major events that happened in this period. As you know, every source is different. How is the information from the website the same as the information in Chapter Three? What new information did you learn?**

### A CENTURY OF HOLLYWOOD EVENTS

**abdocorelibrary.com/hollywood**

# CHAPTER FOUR

# HOLLYWOOD IN TRANSITION

The Great Depression lasted until 1941. In that year, the United States entered World War II (1939–1945). The war affected Hollywood's film industry. A US government agency limited budgets for film sets to $5,000. The government did not want film studios to use more materials than necessary. Materials were needed to build supplies to help with the war effort. Despite this limitation, studios continued to create entertaining films. Beginning in the 1930s, movie theaters showed funny cartoons before movies. In the 1940s, the cartoons promoted

**In the 1930s, filmmakers used special equipment and lighting to make films.**

the war effort. Newsreels shared news footage about the war. They kept people informed.

## PERSPECTIVES

### FILM NOIR

In the 1940s, a new style of filmmaking became popular. Filmmakers used low lighting, flashbacks, and voiceovers to make dramatic stories about crime in America. French film critics later called this style *film noir*. This French phrase means "dark film." The 1941 movie *The Maltese Falcon* is considered to be one of the most important examples of film noir. Film historian Sheri Chinen Biesen said, "These early noir films created a psychological atmosphere that in many ways marked a response to an increasingly realistic and understandable anxiety—about war, shortages . . . and 'a world gone mad.'"

## AFTER THE WAR

For many years, politicians had paid close attention to the content in Hollywood movies. They worried that films were promoting values that were seen as anti-American, such as communism. After World War II ended, politicians targeted

Hollywood. They sought out people they thought were communist.

In 1947, some people were called to testify to Congress on communism in Hollywood. Ten men who were suspected of having communist ties were sent to jail. They were called the Hollywood Ten. Industry leaders blacklisted hundreds of people in the 1950s and 1960s. They thought these people had ties to communism. Those who were blacklisted could not find work in the film industry.

## TELEVISION

Television became widely popular in the 1950s. It changed the way Americans viewed entertainment. Television sets had recently become more affordable. So instead of going to see movies, many people watched TV programs from their own homes. As a result, the number of moviegoers began to decline. Hollywood film studios lost money. To make up for this, they began shooting TV programming as well as films.

There were some big moneymaking movies in the 1950s. These included *The Ten Commandments* and *Around the World in 80 Days*. But many Hollywood companies lost money and talent. Twentieth Century-Fox was forced to sell its backlot in 1956. RKO Radio Pictures closed altogether. But Lucille Ball and her husband bought the studio in 1957. Ball was a television executive, producer, and actress. They named their studio Desilu Productions.

### THE MUSIC INDUSTRY

**By day, musicians recorded music in the Capitol Records Building. Frank Sinatra, Nat King Cole, and the Beatles were some famous musicians who recorded with Capitol Studios. At night, musicians played in clubs in a part of Hollywood called the Sunset Strip. Clubs such as Whisky a Go Go and the Roxy Theatre attracted large crowds. Some of these places are still standing in Hollywood today.**

## MUSIC AND LAUGHS

In addition to television, other entertainment industries came to

Hollywood. Music played a big role in the district's growth. One of the most important developments was the Capitol Records Building. It was built in 1956 on the intersection of Hollywood Boulevard and Vine Street. The building was made to look like a giant stack of records. The building housed the music recording company Capitol Studios.

In the 1960s, stand-up comedy became popular in Hollywood. The comedy club the Laugh Factory opened in 1979. Famous comedians such as Ellen DeGeneres and Jerry Seinfeld performed there.

## ISSUES IN HOLLYWOOD

Hollywood has long been a symbol for success and wealth. But people have also struggled in Hollywood. During Hollywood's Golden Age, drug and alcohol abuse was common. Actors worked long hours. Their work contracts were often strict. Contracts are agreements that determine working conditions. The contracts controlled what stars were allowed to do both

Child star Shirley Temple was harassed and overworked in the 1930s and 1940s.

inside and outside the studio. Many studio executives were powerful men. They sometimes pressured stars to take pills. They thought pills would help power stars through many hours in the studio. Executives also sexually harassed many women.

In the 1970s and 1980s, the crime rate rose in Hollywood. Housing prices also increased as wealthy people settled in the district. Rich people lived in separate neighborhoods from low-income people.

Homelessness has been a problem throughout Hollywood's history. This is still the case today. Displacement and high housing prices contributed to this problem. Like many other US cities, Hollywood is not perfect. It continues to face many challenges.

# STRAIGHT TO THE SOURCE

Nina Ljeti is a former actor turned director. In a 2018 article, she explained how moving to Hollywood had been good for her career:

> *I was never willing to risk anything in my life as an actor, and perhaps that's where my resentment towards the industry came from. But now, I am ready to fight and risk everything to maintain and continue my life as a filmmaker. . . .*
>
> *To me, [Hollywood] will always be a desert valley filled with snake-like highways, where dreams may die and where most of what glitters isn't gold. But [it] is also a place where you are safe, where the possibilities are endless, and where you will always be free to follow your dreams. But only if you choose to see it that way.*

Source: Nina Ljeti. "Why I Walked Away From a Hollywood Acting Career." *Refinery29*. Refinery29, May 1, 2018. Web. Accessed March 25, 2019.

### Point of View

Ljeti thinks there are positive and negative aspects of Hollywood. What does she find inspiring about Hollywood? Read back through this chapter. Do you agree? Why or why not?

# CHAPTER FIVE

# HOLLYWOOD TODAY

Hollywood looks different today than it did in the 1900s. Fancy hotels and stores have replaced some of the nightclubs that closed on the Sunset Strip. Most of the major film studios that were founded in Hollywood have closed or have been bought by other companies. Today, those that remain are not just film studios. They have interests in many different industries.

In the late 2000s, digital media became a major industry in Hollywood. The streaming service Netflix moved its West Coast headquarters to Hollywood in 2017.

**Today, Hollywood remains a popular tourist destination.**

## HOLLYWOOD'S JAZZ MURAL

**Hollywood's historic buildings preserve the district's past. Artist Richard Wyatt created a mural on the south wall of the Capitol Records Building. This mural was unveiled in 1990. It is called *Hollywood Jazz: 1945–1972*. It shows legendary jazz musicians such as Miles Davis, Ella Fitzgerald, and Nat King Cole. These musicians helped influence Hollywood's music industry. In 2011, the deteriorating mural was restored. Wyatt used 2,288 ceramic tiles to recreate the image so it would be around for years to come.**

The technology company Amazon also has a presence in Hollywood. It has used old film studio lots to film TV shows.

## #OSCARSSOWHITE

Today, Hollywood plays an important role in social movements. One of these movements is called #OscarsSoWhite. This movement encourages the Academy Awards to consider more people of color for Oscar awards. The #OscarsSoWhite movement began in 2015. In that year, all 20 of the actors and actresses nominated

# DIVERSITY
## IN HOLLYWOOD

Hollywood is sometimes called the birthplace of movies. But it is often easier for some people to get into the film industry than others. This graph shows the percentages of women and minorities in film industry roles in 2018. Which categories have the lowest numbers? How do you think the film industry could address these issues?

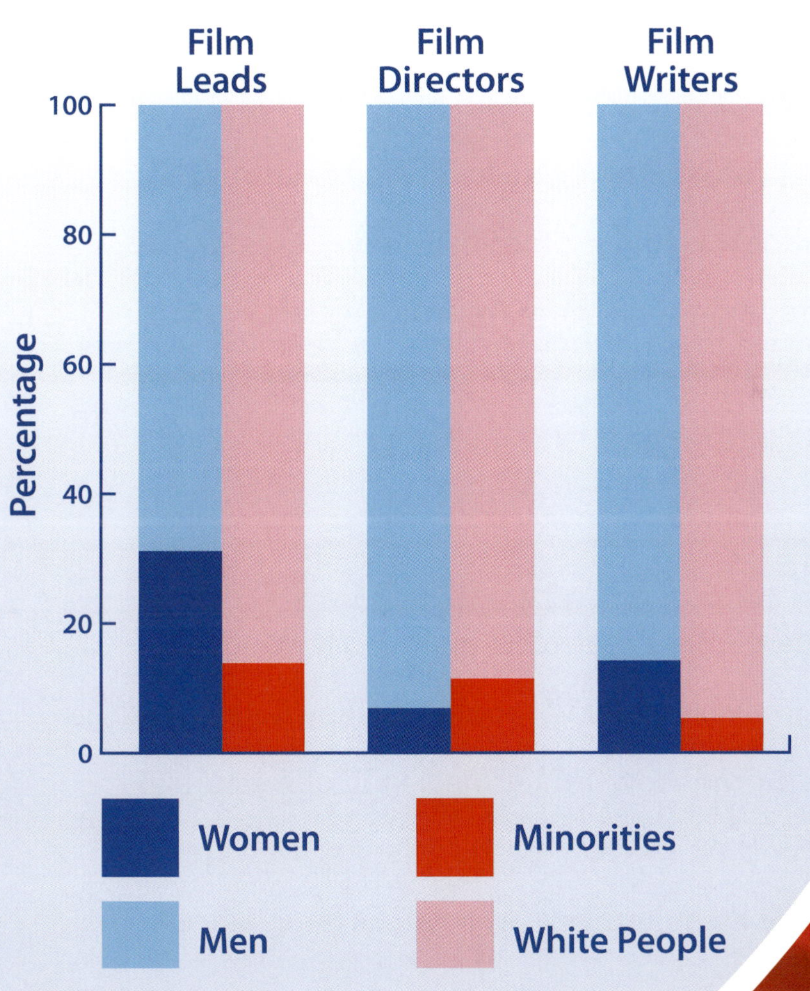

for the lead and supporting acting categories were white. Many people were frustrated by this lack of diversity. Activist April Reign created the Twitter hashtag #OscarsSoWhite. She wanted to make the world more aware of this problem.

In 2016, all of the Academy Award nominees for the lead and supporting acting categories were once again white. Some celebrities refused to attend the Academy Awards in protest. The #OscarsSoWhite hashtag became widely popular on social media. In response to this campaign, Academy Awards officials voted to double the number of women and minorities in their organization by 2020.

## #METOO

Another movement that took off in Hollywood is #MeToo. In October 2017, actress Ashley Judd wrote an article for the *New York Times*. In it, she said film producer and Academy member Harvey Weinstein had sexually assaulted her. Two weeks later, actress

Alyssa Milano urged sexual assault survivors to tweet "#MeToo" on Twitter. Millions of people responded. #MeToo quickly gained momentum as a movement.

On November 12, 2017, thousands of people participated in a #MeToo demonstration in Hollywood. They marched in support of victims of sexual assault and harassment. The protest started near the Dolby Theatre. The participants marched for one mile (1.6 km). Activist Tarana Burke organized the march. Burke and other women gave speeches.

## PERSPECTIVES

### TARANA BURKE

**Today's #MeToo movement can be traced back to 2006. In that year, activist Tarana Burke used the phrase "Me too" to spread the word about sexual assault. She supported girls and women of color who were sexual assault survivors. She wanted to raise awareness of this problem. In 2017, Burke helped expand the movement's reach beyond Hollywood. In an interview, she said, "The conversation around harassment in Hollywood will broaden to include other industries if we force it to. It's not going to do it on its own."**

**Tarana Burke, *middle*, and other sexual assault survivors marched along Hollywood Boulevard in 2017 to raise awareness of #MeToo.**

## LOOKING AHEAD

Many people in Hollywood are working to address issues in the film industry. Activists hope to fix the industry's lack of racial diversity. They also work to empower and hire more women.

In 2019, more than 146,000 people lived in Hollywood. More than 6 million people visit the district each year. For these people and many other Americans, Hollywood remains a place of hope and progress.

# STRAIGHT TO THE SOURCE

April Reign created the #OscarsSoWhite hashtag in 2015. She wrote an article about the movement for *Vanity Fair* magazine in 2018. She explained that there was still more work to be done to solve Hollywood's diversity problem. She wrote:

> *Finding diverse talent might appear to be challenging, but it is only if studios rely on their traditional network, or assume that the usual handful of bankable white stars can carry a film. Hollywood must be forward-thinking enough to pivot as the market demands. . . . Until we can no longer count on our fingers the number of nominations drawn from historically overlooked segments of society, #OscarsSoWhite remains relevant. The struggle continues.*

Source: April Reign. "#OscarsSoWhite Is Still Relevant This Year." *Vanity Fair.* Vanity Fair, March 2, 2018. Web. Accessed June 24, 2019.

### Consider Your Audience

Adapt this passage for a different audience, such as your friends. Write a blog post conveying this same information for the new audience. How does your post differ from the original text and why?

# IMPORTANT DATES

**1887**
Harvey and Daeida Wilcox divide up some of their land in California's Cahuenga Valley. This land becomes Hollywood.

**1903**
Hollywood becomes an official town.

**1910**
Hollywood merges with Los Angeles. It becomes a district in Los Angeles. More than 5,000 people live in Hollywood at this time.

**1911**
The first Hollywood film is made.

**1927**
*The Jazz Singer*, the first talking feature film, is released. The Academy of Motion Picture Arts and Sciences is founded.

**1947–1960s**
The Hollywood blacklist period makes it difficult for many people to find employment in the film industry.

**2015**

Activist April Reign creates the hashtag #OscarsSoWhite.

**2017**

Thousands of people participate in a #MeToo march in Hollywood.

# STOP AND THINK

## Say What?

Studying a historic location can mean learning a lot of new vocabulary. Find five words in this book you've never seen before. Use a dictionary to find out what they mean. Then write the meanings in your own words, and use each word in a new sentence.

## Surprise Me

Chapter Three explores Hollywood's Golden Age. After reading this book, what two or three facts about this period did you find most surprising? Write a few sentences about each fact. Why did you find each fact surprising?

## Take a Stand

This book discusses the lack of diversity in the film industry. The #OscarsSoWhite movement was created in response to this issue. Do you think people outside of Hollywood could help address this problem? Why or why not? What are some ways people could try to fix this problem?

## You Are There

This book describes some of Hollywood's most popular tourist attractions. Imagine you are a travel blogger. Write a blog post about your first trip to Hollywood. Be sure to include details about some of the places you visited and facts you learned about the city's history.

# GLOSSARY

**backlot**
an area behind a film studio that is used to create sets and scenes

**communism**
the belief that the ownership of all goods should be shared

**district**
an area or region within a larger city

**diversity**
the state of having people of different races and backgrounds together in one place

**documentary**
a movie that covers real-life events

**harassment**
a type of behavior that is meant to threaten or harm someone

**mission**
a local church that is supported by a larger religious group

**nominate**
to consider someone for an award

**plaque**
a flat piece of material, usually metal or wood, that is meant to honor or remember something

**stand-up comedy**
a type of act in which a person tells jokes in front of an audience

# ONLINE RESOURCES

To learn more about Hollywood, visit our free resource websites below.

Visit **abdocorelibrary.com** or scan this QR code for free Common Core resources for teachers and students, including vetted activities, multimedia, and booklinks, for deeper subject comprehension.

Visit **abdobooklinks.com** or scan this QR code for free additional online weblinks for further learning. These links are routinely monitored and updated to provide the most current information available.

# LEARN MORE

Anastasio, Dina. *Where Is Hollywood?* New York: Penguin Workshop, 2019.

Hamilton, John. *California: The Golden State.* Minneapolis, MN: Abdo Publishing, 2017.

# INDEX



## About the Author


Alexis Burling has written dozens of articles and books for young readers on a variety of topics, including current events, nutrition, US history, and biographies. She is also a book critic with reviews and interviews published in the *New York Times*, *San Francisco Chronicle*, and more. She lives with her husband in the mountainous Pacific Northwest.